Christina, The Girl King

Also by Michel Marc Bouchard

The Coronation Voyage*

Down Dangerous Passes Road*

Heat Wave

Lilies

The Madonna Painter*

The Orphan Muses

The Tale of Teeka*

Tom at the Farm*

Written on Water*

Available from Talonbooks

Christina, The Girl King

MICHEL MARC BOUCHARD

TRANSLATED BY LINDA GABORIAU

TALONBOOKS

Talonbooks
278 East First Avenue, Vancouver, British Columbia, Canada v5t 1a6
www.talonbooks.com

First printing: 2014

Typeset in Adobe Garamond
Printed and bound in Canada on 100% post-consumer recycled paper
Interior and cover design by Typesmith

On the cover: *Christina, Queen of Sweden* by Achille Devéria, printed by François Le Villain, published by Edward Bull, published by Edward Churton, after Sébastien Bourdon hand-coloured lithograph, 1830s (National Portrait Gallery, London)

Talonbooks gratefully acknowledges the financial support of the Canada Council for the Arts, the Government of Canada through the Canada Book Fund, and the Province of British Columbia through the British Columbia Arts Council and the Book Publishing Tax Credit.

This work was originally published in French as *Christine, la reine-garçon* by Leméac Éditeur in 2012. The English translation was commissioned by the Stratford Shakespeare Festival, in Stratford, Ontario.

Rights to produce *Christina, The Girl King*, in whole or in part, in any medium by any group, amateur or professional, are retained by the author. Interested persons are requested to contact his agent: Goodwin Agency, Suite 200, 839 Sherbrooke Street East, Montreal, Quebec h2l 1k6; tel.: (514) 598-5252; www.agencegoodwin.com.

Library and Archives Canada Cataloguing in Publication

Bouchard, Michel Marc, 1958–
[Christine, la reine-garçon. English]
        Christina, the girl king / Michel Marc Bouchard ;
translated by Linda Gaboriau.

A play.
Translation of: Christine, la reine-garçon.
Issued in print and electronic formats.
isbn 978-0-88922-898-6 (pbk.).—isbn 978-0-88922-899-3 (epub)

        1. Christina, Queen of Sweden, 1626–1689—Drama. I. Gaboriau, Linda, translator II. Title.

ps8553.o7745c4713 2014   c842'.54   c2014-902787-7
                                                c2014-902788-5

To Linda Gaboriau,
my ally in all the battles.

To Anna Stratton,
who introduced me to Christina of Sweden.

*We try in vain to appear to be
what we are not.*

Christina, Queen of Sweden

PREFACE

Christina of Sweden is fascinating because she is so modern.
An enigmatic queen, flamboyant and unpredictable, a
woman eager for knowledge, a tomboy, a feminist before her
time, she wreaked havoc throughout northern Europe in the
mid-seventeenth century.

She is six years old when her father, the great defender of
the Lutheran faith, dies, leaving her to reign over an empire
she hopes to make the most sophisticated in all of Europe.

She wants to control everything, yet she cannot master
her own feelings—the ones she dares not name, the ones
that defy reason—including that strange love, the love that,
to this very day, her biographers fail to name.

To fulfill her personal aspirations, with extraordinary
political shrewdness, she manages to cast off the yoke
imposed by her faith and her title.

I have chosen to write a classical play, in the
longstanding tradition of theatre written to portray heroes.
I have tried to examine the question that Christina of
Sweden raises, the question more relevant today than ever:
how to choose between the common good and personal
aspirations. Between one's country and oneself.

Was Christina a heroine of the cause for individual
freedom or a traitor to her country?

Christina of Sweden renounced the country she loved, renounced her father, her faith, everything she was in order to become what she wanted to be: free to define herself, using her "free will," in keeping with the teachings of her friend René Descartes.

Michel Marc Bouchard
AUGUST 31, 2012

PRODUCTION HISTORY

Christine, la reine-garçon premiered on November 15, 2012, at Théâtre du Nouveau Monde in Montreal, Quebec, under the artistic direction of Lorraine Pintal, in a production directed by Serge Denoncourt, assisted by Elaine Normandeau, with the following cast and creative team:

Catherine Bégin: MARIA ELEONORA OF BRANDENBURG
Céline Bonnier: CHRISTINA, QUEEN OF SWEDEN
David Boutin: GENERALISSIMO KARL GUSTAV
Éric Bruneau: COUNT JOHAN OXENSTIERNA
Louise Cardinal: DUCHESS ERIKA BRÄHE
Jean-François Casabonne: RENÉ DESCARTES
Mathieu Handfield: THE ALBINO
Robert Lalonde: CHANCELLOR AXEL OXENSTIERNA
Magalie Lépine-Blondeau: COUNTESS EBBA SPARRE
Gabriel Sabourin: CHANUT

SET DESIGNER: Guillaume Lord
COSTUME DESIGNER: François Barbeau
LIGHTING DESIGNER: Martin Labrecque
MAKEUP ARTIST: Amélie Bruno-Longpré
MUSIC AND SOUND DESIGNER: Philip Pinsky

The English-language version of the play, *Christina, The Girl King*, was originally commissioned by the Stratford Shakespeare Festival of Stratford, Ontario, and premiered there on August 14, 2014, under the artistic direction of Antoni Cimolino and the executive direction of Anita Gaffney, in a production directed by Vanessa Porteous, with the following cast and creative team:

Graham Abbey: COUNT JOHAN OXENSTIERNA

Wayne Best: CHANCELLOR AXEL OXENSTIERNA

Kevin Bundy: CHANUT

Patricia Collins: MARIA ELEONORA OF BRANDENBURG

John Kirkpatrick: RENÉ DESCARTES

Claire Lautier: COUNTESS EBBA SPARRE

Elliott Loran: THE ALBINO

Rylan Wilkie: GENERALISSIMO KARL GUSTAV

Brigit Wilson: DUCHESS ERIKA BRÄHE

Jenny Young: CHRISTINA, QUEEN OF SWEDEN

DESIGNER: Michael Gianfrancesco

LIGHTING DESIGNER: Kimberly Purtell

MUSIC AND SOUND DESIGNER: Alexander MacSween

DRAMATURGE: Bob White

FIGHT DIRECTOR: John Stead

ASSISTANT DIRECTOR: Jessica Carmichael

ASSISTANT COSTUME DESIGNER: Alyssa Westman

STAGE MANAGER: Melissa Rood

ASSISTANT STAGE MANAGERS:

    Renate Hanson, Christopher Sibbald

PRODUCTION STAGE MANAGER: Michael Hart

TECHNICAL DIRECTOR: Robbin Cheesman

CHARACTERS

(in order of appearance)

DUCHESS ERIKA BRÄHE
    Second lady-in-waiting to the queen

COUNTESS EBBA SPARRE
    First lady-in-waiting to the queen

CHRISTINA
    Queen of Sweden

GENERALISSIMO KARL GUSTAV
    Christina's cousin

CHANCELLOR AXEL OXENSTIERNA
    Chancellor of Sweden

COUNT JOHAN OXENSTIERNA
    Axel's son

CHANUT
    France's ambassador to Sweden

RENÉ DESCARTES
    French philosopher

MARIA ELEONORA OF BRANDENBURG
    Christina's mother and widow of King Gustav II

THE ALBINO

THE CADAVER

Part One

Mid-seventeenth century. Sweden. Uppsala Castle. Winter.

Erika and Ebba appear in a spotlight. Ebba is holding two crystal goblets. She listens anxiously as Erika tells her story.

ERIKA. It happened suddenly. The queen was in high spirits, a mood all too rare for her. It was infectious. Even the echo of her cursing spread good humour throughout the court. I remember the moon was full and cast long, generous shadows. It was a misleading moon. We didn't see the dark wall approaching in the distance. A wall of deep, murky grey. And the queen's happy cursing masked the silence about to descend on us. The chancellor and his son, and the ambassador of France and his philosopher, they were all there. And the queen's cousin, Karl Gustav. The sleighs raced over frozen Lake Malar. The reindeer were hard to control. Their instinct must have alerted them to what was about to happen. And the snow, the wind. The sky had released its fury on us.

Ebba disappears.

1. THE TROPHY ROOM

The walls are decorated with hunting trophies displaying an impressive array of antlers.

Christina enters, followed by Karl Gustav, Chancellor Axel Oxenstierna, and his son, Johan. Their greatcoats are dripping with snow. Erika goes to help Christina remove her coat, but Christina pushes her away so brusquely that she almost falls. Erika catches her balance and curtseys. Chanut and Descartes join the group.

KARL GUSTAV. (*kneeling, on the verge of tears*) I recognize the gravity of my mistake! I am prepared for the punishment.

CHRISTINA. You hurt me.

KARL GUSTAV. Forgive me!

CHRISTINA. You hurt my shoulder.

KARL GUSTAV. I'm crying.

CHRISTINA. I didn't grant you permission to cry.

KARL GUSTAV. I beg you to forgive me.

CHRISTINA. I didn't grant you permission to whine.

KARL GUSTAV. You must realize that my offence is born of my all-too-great affection for you.

CHRISTINA. My cousin, certainly you can feel affection for me without succumbing to such outbursts! Should you dare look into a mirror, you will be appalled by the appearance of the chief of my armies!

KARL GUSTAV. After everything I did for you! Twenty thousand men led by my voice. For Queen Christina!

For *Drottning* Christina! I brought you the treasures of Bohemia. The Caravaggios! The Michelangelos! The Raphaels! The wealth of the Holy German Empire! The alchemy notebooks of Emperor Rudolf. All the books from Poland's monasteries.

CHRISTINA. And?!

KARL GUSTAV. Every blow I struck, every one of my shouts, every one of my wounds bore your name. Twenty thousand men to take Prague!

CHRISTINA. And? Am I supposed to thank you by sacrificing my honour?

KARL GUSTAV. Once you said you loved me.

CHRISTINA. I was twelve years old.

KARL GUSTAV. You said I was your fiancé.

CHRISTINA. At twelve, everyone is our fiancé.

KARL GUSTAV. I whispered sweet nothings in your ear. You loved my gentle voice. One day, I touched your lips with my fingertips. If my love overflows in my eyes and my gestures, if this feeling I can't control angers you, I will never forgive myself. I love you! I love you! I love you!

CHRISTINA. You're repeating yourself, like a puppy lapping up a puddle.

KARL GUSTAV. And I'll repeat it again. I love you. I love you. I love you.

CHRISTINA. By St. Agatha's severed breasts! You threw yourself on me like an animal. In the middle of the blizzard. Sweating, salivating. Grunting, drooling.

You were brutal. Like a bear. Your foul breath. Your
greasy paws. Obeying that incubus between your legs,
you pinned me to the ground. Your sovereign, on the
ground. Your reason for living, on the ground.

KARL GUSTAV. It was the wind.

CHRISTINA. (*to everyone*) And no one came to my rescue!
No one answered my cries for help.

AXEL. The snow masked everything.

JOHAN. The howling wind drowned every sound.

AXEL. I lost my bearings.

JOHAN. Impossible to set one foot before the other.

AXEL. I lost all sense of where I was.

CHRISTINA. If I hadn't fought him off, he would have
impregnated me like a sow. That would have solved
Sweden's biggest problem!

Beat.

KARL GUSTAV. The wind toppled us over. The blizzard
made you imagine things. It was only an embrace.
An adoring embrace. I longed to take you in my arms.
And hold you tight. To breathe you in and feel you
pressed against me. My reason for living, pressed against
me. Do you know what it's like to long for the smell and
feel of someone?

CHRISTINA. No one can touch me!

KARL GUSTAV. (*disarmingly sincere*) Christina! Marry me!

Christina slaps him.

CHRISTINA. By Christ's bleeding wounds! Not marriage, again! Yesterday, Philip of Spain asked for my hand! An incurable syphilitic who preys on virgins! He wrote that he would make me deeply happy! Tomorrow will bring a messenger from the dauphin of Denmark! I'm told he will pay grandiloquent homage to me. By God's ass, I doubt that he is the author of this praise. He's only three years old. Am I so desirable? So irresistible? Tell me! Is it my bulging eyes that inspire such passion?

KARL GUSTAV. Don't say that!

CHRISTINA. Do my asymmetrical shoulders inspire these ballads? Is it my curses and tantrums that arouse such tenderness?

KARL GUSTAV. Don't say that!

CHRISTINA. I know my true worth, but I am not unaware of my appearance. Marriage entails a submissiveness I cannot envisage, nor can I foresee the day when I will overcome this repulsion. I cannot accept the idea that a man could exploit me the way a peasant plows his fields. I know that someday I will have to submit to this fate. I am aware of my duty. But for the time being, I have other plans. I inherited from my father a country of miners and lumberjacks, peasants and soldiers who find contentment in two mugs of beer and travelling carnival acts. Illiteracy is rampant. Ignorance is the lot of the lower classes. People make fun of intellectuals. They are suspicious of learning. Our upper classes cannot quote a single author and their knowledge of *les belles lettres* is limited to the alphabet. Everyone can sing a song, but no one reads. Everyone can count, but no one thinks. My people have no choice but to believe what they're told to believe, and to repeat it dutifully.

My people have no words, no ideas, and if they had ideas, they wouldn't have the words to express them. We need schools, libraries, scholars, poets. I want to make my country the most sophisticated country in the world. We must welcome the thinkers who are persecuted for their ideas so they can enlighten us. And to achieve that, for now, we must put aside effusive sentimentality and the bloody business of childbirth.

KARL GUSTAV. I love you all the more.

CHRISTINA. Chancellor!

AXEL. Madam?

CHRISTINA. Tend to the arrangements for my cousin's departure!

KARL GUSTAV. Am I leaving?

CHRISTINA. For Finland.

KARL GUSTAV. I can't live without you.

CHRISTINA. A palace. One hundred servants. You will recover.

KARL GUSTAV. I'll hold my breath until we are reunited.

Christina exits, followed by Erika.

KARL GUSTAV. (*to the others*) It was the wind.

He exits.

AXEL. (*coolly*) Are you enjoying our court, Monsieur Descartes?

DESCARTES. The food is atrocious, and so is the excuse for wine you serve. Your staff are as welcoming as jailors. The cold is so intense, it freezes your tongue the minute

6

you open your mouth to say, "The cold is so intense, it freezes my tongue the minute I open my mouth to say, 'The cold is so intense'!"

AXEL. (*turning to Chanut*) *Monsieur l'ambassadeur.* Manners at the Louvre are undoubtedly more refined, but ours have the virtue of being frank and lively.

CHANUT. "By St. Agatha's severed breasts"! Your queen uses colourful language.

JOHAN. She speaks seven others. Fluently.

CHANUT. "Impregnated like a sow"?

AXEL. When she was born, her first cry was so deep, her body so hairy that all of Sweden believed that the baby was a boy. Her mother's repeated miscarriages and the dashed hopes for a prince had misled everyone. A boy! The rumour travelled more quickly than a wild stallion. A boy! Up and down the hallways. A boy! Pages ran to inform the king too soon. At last, he had a son! A salvo of cannon shots announced the arrival of a dauphin. Then came the time to present the girl to the king. She was wrapped in swaddling clothes and I took her to her father myself. When he unwrapped the child: "A girl?! How clever of her! How mischievous already! She fooled us! This girl will prove to be as worthy as any boy. We were expecting a prince, we shall raise her as the greatest prince of all."

CHANUT. There is no denying it, Chancellor, our monarchies are very different.

AXEL. True. Ours is founded on a consensus between all the constituent bodies of our nation. Yours is the result of some "holy" oil, carried by some dove to anoint the forehead of some saint named Louis. We don't indulge in this amusing penchant for fantasy. No, *monsieur*! We prefer to vote.

DESCARTES. The queen delivered a courageous plea in favour of curiosity and knowledge.

JOHAN. Yes. She is very courageous when it comes to defending her celibacy. Every time her hymen is threatened, instead of calling for help, she calls for "scholars, schools, libraries"!

AXEL. (*reprimanding him*) My son!

JOHAN. (*resigned*) Yes, a fine plea. Very fine.

DESCARTES. She acted of her own free will.

JOHAN. Free will?

DESCARTES. Our ability to determine our destiny ourselves.

AXEL. Luther, our spiritual guide, teaches that God alone determines our destiny.

DESCARTES. Unlike Luther, I believe that we can determine our lives ourselves. In a constant dialogue with God. We are just beginning to understand that it might be the earth that gravitates around the sun. We are beginning to recognize that what we called the finite universe might be infinite, and consequently, the God we had defined might be indefinable.

AXEL. Those are rash thoughts.

DESCARTES. A new world is unfolding before us.

AXEL. Our queen's curiosity is boundless. One speaks to her of the moon, she becomes an astrologer. Mention a single flower and she turns to botany. Despite her apparent confidence, she could be attracted by the mirages offered by your Church, so quick to tear up pages of the Scriptures to satisfy the whims of princes.

CHANUT. I cannot respond to these declarations now. These matters were not part of our protocol.

AXEL. Can you hear the wind over our moors? The night? The blizzard driving the snow?

JOHAN. (*in a ghoulish tone*) Death to all Catholics!

AXEL. The lamentations of the souls of our fathers, our brothers, our sons?

JOHAN. (*in a ghoulish tone*) Burn the pope at the stake!

AXEL. The plaintive cry of those who fought against your papists?

JOHAN. (*in a ghoulish tone*) Down with Rome!

AXEL. You can empty our mines, cut down our forests. But make sure that the earth remains the centre of the universe, God, the centre of our lives, and Luther, our guiding light. And make sure you keep your philosopher on a leash.

CHANUT. According to our protocol, this exchange never took place.

AXEL. According to your protocol.

CHANUT and DESCARTES. Gentlemen.

Chanut and Descartes bow and exit.

AXEL. She has invited the Devil into our home. She mystifies me.

Beat.

JOHAN. I love my legs. I've always loved my legs. I love
their length. I find them appealing. I believe the length
of a man's legs is what matters. Women stare at them
when I pass by. Then they look at my face. Always the
same movement, from the bottom up. You should see
how embarrassed they are, Father! And deceitful. They
try to hide the emotion my arrival arouses in them.
I don't know if I'm handsome, but I'm seductive. There's
something in the way I move. I'm graceful, like a stag.
And the sound of my boots. My beautiful boots. I refuse
to reveal the name of my boot maker. Sometimes
I seduce myself, Father, I swear I do. All the dwarves in
this court who try so desperately to grow taller. (*beat*)
I love my thighs, too.

AXEL. (*exasperated*) JOHAN! If only grace could reach your
brain and guide the movement from the top down, I'd
have reason to be proud of you.

JOHAN. I thought Karl Gustav was going to succeed. At the
height of the blizzard, I told him, "This is your chance!
Even though the queen is your cousin, even though we
loathe inbreeding, this is your chance! She's not pretty.
Your children will be ugly. But, this is your chance! Your
love for her is real. You have everything it takes to melt
her icy heart. This is your chance!" Without warning,
he threw himself on her. (*He imitates Karl Gustav.*)
"I love you! I love you! I love you!" The sobbing bear has
a pathetic heart and weeping genitals.

AXEL. The vulgarity of youth is disarming.

JOHAN. Our monarchy is dull enough to put stones to
sleep. Not the slightest shadow of a crime. No trace of
murderous intrigue. Not a single portrait reveals the
traits of a despot. Variations on monotony adorn our

walls. Bloodless faces and glassy eyes wondering what they did to deserve to hang there forever. Is that all we can hope for? We had war to distract us. Christina wants peace! We had torture to educate us. Christina wants to forbid it. How will we be able to distinguish true from false? A civilized country tortures, for God's sake! Enemies are our livelihood. How will we quench our soldiers' thirst for battle? It's high time a man brought her to her senses! Feeling a man between her legs should become the subject of our Majesty's curiosity. Let her cease to be a brain and become a belly. And if she dies in childbirth, at least she will have tried to assume her duty.

AXEL. How dare you speak of your sister like that!

JOHAN. My "sister"! Your affection for her will be your downfall.

AXEL. You grew up together.

JOHAN. You might have raised her since her father's death, you might have looked after her day and night, at the expense of your own son, but that doesn't make her my sister. Consider her your daughter if it suits you—

AXEL. It suits me, my son, it suits me.

JOHAN. We can only hope an orgasm will soon send a rush of royal blood to her brain and eliminate her revolutionary fantasies. A man between her legs. You hear me! A man between her legs!

Johan goes to leave.

AXEL. And why not you?

JOHAN. Why not me?

AXEL. She has always enjoyed your company.

JOHAN. Me? On the throne? Are you serious?

AXEL. You always got along well.

JOHAN. In fencing. And on horseback. We always got along. And at bear hunting, too. Like brothers, Father. Like brothers.

AXEL. I think it's high time your long legs served the kingdom.

They exit.

2. THE SAME SETTING

Descartes and Christina enter the empty room, followed by Erika, who sits down at a distance and attempts to read a book. Christina is rubbing her shoulder.

DESCARTES. On the way to your palace, I saw so many forests, and here, on your hearth, so few logs.

CHRISTINA. We will meet every day.

DESCARTES. Every day.

CHRISTINA. Every morning!

DESCARTES. Every morning!

CHRISTINA. At five o'clock!

DESCARTES. At five o'clock.

CHRISTINA. Yes, that's when my mind is most alert. You're making a face?

DESCARTES. Because of my shoes. They're new. No, because of the cold! No, because of five o'clock in the morning!

CHRISTINA. I'll be brief. I brought you to Sweden for two reasons. The first: I want you to explain what love is.

DESCARTES. And the second?

CHRISTINA. How to get rid of it! (*beat*) Not long ago, I think I experienced this feeling for the first time. I still don't understand what draws us to one person rather than another, even before we know that person's worth. Where does this insidious attraction originate? In the body or in the mind?

DESCARTES. Love is an emotion that incites the soul to connect with objects that appear suitable.

CHRISTINA. Go on.

DESCARTES. There are two distinct kinds of love. One is called compassionate love, a love that incites us to wish the best for what we love.

CHRISTINA. And the other?

DESCARTES. Concupiscent love.

CHRISTINA. Meaning?

DESCARTES. It incites the soul to desire what we love.

CHRISTINA. And how can we distinguish between the two?

DESCARTES. Every passion transforms us physically, and each has its own symptoms. We can recognize them by changes in pulse and in breathing or by variations in the colour of our skin.

CHRISTINA. If I tremble like a leaf, if I become red as a Dane, does that betray my feelings?

DESCARTES. To anyone who can read the signs, yes.

CHRISTINA. What about the expressions on my face?

DESCARTES. The face is deceitful. It is hard to distinguish its motives, since we can wilfully change its expressions. To hide one passion, we can imagine another, its exact opposite.

CHRISTINA. Tell me more about the love you call concupiscent.

DESCARTES. Under its spell, we feel a pleasant warmth in the chest. Our complexion becomes flushed because of the rush of blood. Our heartbeats are longer and louder than usual, and our stomach can more readily digest meat. As a result, this passion is considered beneficial for our health.

CHRISTINA. How can we be sure not to confuse the two kinds of love?

DESCARTES. (*observing Christina closely*) Short, rapid breath. Decidedly flushed skin. I believe, *madame*, that you know how to distinguish the two.

CHRISTINA. Recently, a passion has been disturbing me and diverting me from my destiny. I thought that given my rank, only God had power over me. And here I am, under the yoke of someone my inferior. This disturbance is distracting me from matters of state. I understand Pascal's hydrostatic experiments and Kepler's theory on the elliptical trajectory of the planets, but I can't explain this new agitation. For a moment of stolen pleasure, my mind wanders and I forget the important points of the decree at hand. I become as foolish as a page who dreams of nothing but grazing an elbow or a knee. The sensation that my chest is on fire is bothersome. And I'm afraid I must contradict you. I have no appetite for a leg of mutton or a stew. Tell me how I can escape this tyranny.

DESCARTES. My philosophy does not deny the usefulness of passions. On the contrary, I believe that happiness and life's finest pleasures can reside in them.

CHRISTINA. Your knowledge of emotions is said to be unsurpassed, and you have no solution?

DESCARTES. Instead of submitting to them, we have to understand them and tame them. I believe that we are free to determine our lives. To act and think on our own. To distinguish good from evil, and all of this, in a dialogue with God.

CHRISTINA. Your views are disturbing, Monsieur Descartes.

DESCARTES. I recently discovered a gland, a tiny gland, no bigger than a pine nut, located in the middle of our brain. It is the meeting place of body and mind. It is where feelings of joy or sadness, hatred or love, are born. This gland might well be the seat of the soul and the soul might not be of divine essence alone.

CHRISTINA. (*horrified*) How can you claim such a thing?

DESCARTES. If we could understand the workings of this gland the way we understand the circulation of blood or the reaction of nerves, we could—

CHRISTINA. We could exercise control over our passions?

DESCARTES. Perhaps.

CHRISTINA. Remove a clot of hatred. A slice of desire?

DESCARTES. Perhaps.

CHRISTINA. A hemorrhage of anger?

DESCARTES. Why not?

CHRISTINA. Excise love?

DESCARTES. I need cadavers.

CHRISTINA. What?

DESCARTES. I need cadavers for my research.

CHRISTINA. This is madness! The idea that a pine nut in
    our head could challenge the natural order of things.
    Or even worse, divine order. Aristotle wondered whether
    the soul might be made of bone, St. Augustine dared
    venture that it might be made of imprecise material,
    but no one dared hypothesize that it could be a precise
    organ. You could be burned at the stake, here and
    abroad. I ask you to rid me of love, to restore my reason,
    and you respond with nonsensical babble and ask for
    cadavers! (*She feels pain in her shoulder.*) Ay! I get carried
    away and it hurts. By God's ass, it hurts! Karl Gustav
    revived the old injury.

DESCARTES. May I see?

CHRISTINA. A childhood accident. A staircase. A distracted
    servant.

*Descartes touches the queen's shoulder. Erika panics and bolts
up from her chair.*

ERIKA. You can't touch the queen!

CHRISTINA. No one can touch me, *monsieur.*

Descartes removes his hand.

DESCARTES. Wanting to touch you is the message my eyes transmitted to that gland in my brain and my soul judged that this action was beneficial and ordered my hand to touch you gently.

CHRISTINA. It's all very complicated!

DESCARTES. Observation shapes our thoughts. Love now! You can reason later.

Axel enters.

AXEL. (*gravely, to Descartes*) Why wasn't I informed of this meeting? I thought your meetings were to take place at five in the morning?

DESCARTES. (*studying Axel*) Flushed temples. Constricted breath. Contracted iris. Frustration! A feeling related to anger and disappointment. (*bowing*) *Monsieur.* Your Majesty.

CHRISTINA. Tomorrow at five.

DESCARTES. Tomorrow at five.

Erika leads Descartes to the door.

AXEL. (*scolding Christina*) "He who does what he pleases rarely does what he should." When the students at the Lutheran college in Stockholm heard of his arrival at court, they protested in the streets. There are threats on your guest's life.

CHRISTINA. See to his protection!

AXEL. Beware of him. Beware of that ambassador. A Jesuit. Always looking to recruit new Catholics. Their faith is founded on icons and relics. One of St. John the Baptist's bones can buy you a hundred years in paradise.

A thread from Mary Magdalene's skirt, and you
can avoid two centuries in purgatory. Their prelates
grow wealthy from the speculation and fabrication
of these trinkets. Heaven, hell, and purgatory are
the gold standards of the economic system they've
invented. There are so many relics of the Holy Cross
in circulation, they could build a fleet of sailing ships
with them! And so many pieces of the Christ child's
foreskin, I hate to imagine the size of the holy member!
(*Christina smiles.*) The construction of St. Peter's Basilica
has become the pretext for amassing fortunes that
allow their demonic clerical hierarchy to live a life of
greed. Their elastic theology can be adjusted to fit the
highest bidder. Beware! I want to make you the greatest
Lutheran monarch in the world. I've been working
day and night to have your reforms approved, despite
opposition from all quarters. Your dreams are expensive
and peace does not fill the coffers. I believe in your
ideas, so you must help me. Stop allowing your curiosity
to distract you.

CHRISTINA. Your concern is touching, my friend.

AXEL. Your friend?

CHRISTINA. Monsieur Descartes suggests that I make room
for my feelings.

AXEL. Those lace cuffs are new! Has someone found favour
in your eyes?

CHRISTINA. No one, from the court's point of view.
Spanish. The lace.

AXEL. Spanish lace. Italian paintings. French philosophers.
Catholic Europe is courting you.

CHRISTINA. (*annoyed*) Couldn't you simply have said that the lace is beautiful?

AXEL. People said the Trojan Horse was beautiful.

CHRISTINA. The evening prayer. Then leave me alone.

AXEL. (*praying*) "Nature can be devious in matters of desire and one cannot be too vigilant. Lord, let doubt and discernment be my guides."

CHRISTINA. "Lord, let doubt and discernment be my guides."

AXEL. Amen.

CHRISTINA. Amen.

AXEL. Good night, my daughter.

Axel bows and exits. The music of someone making crystal goblets sing.

3. THE QUEEN'S BEDROOM

Tall mullioned windows form an immense semicircle. An impressive bed with a red satin canopy is covered with manuscripts, maps, and diagrams. Ebba, the queen's first lady-in-waiting, an exquisite beauty, is playing a pretty melody by gliding her finger over the rims of crystal goblets placed on a table off to one side.

CHRISTINA. Teach me how!

EBBA. You moisten your finger and place it on the rim of the glass. Then you move it in circles. Each glass produces a different note. The notes change depending upon the amount of water in the glass. (*Christina puts her finger in her mouth to moisten it.*) Wait. (*Ebba shows her how to dip her finger in the water.*) That's better. (*Christina plays several notes.*) When I heard that you were caught in that storm, my heart stopped beating. They told me that you had fallen. I thought of a wild animal. Or even worse, a fanatic. You must be more careful. I was so worried. You seem to enjoy seeing me in this state. Tell me, "I'm fine"!

CHRISTINA. A gust of wind toppled poor Karl Gustav over onto me. I'm fine, Countess Sparre, I'm fine.

EBBA. Your cousin loves you so much.

CHRISTINA. When people love too much, their ridiculous behaviour spoils their charm. I fell on my shoulder.

EBBA. On your good shoulder or the bad one?

CHRISTINA. The bad one.

EBBA. (*delighted*) Lace cuffs?!

CHRISTINA. Your insistence was effective.

Erika enters holding a gown and a small box.

ERIKA. They delivered this gown. A present from a Venetian prince.

CHRISTINA. Look in the sleeve. You'll find another marriage proposal.

EBBA. How audacious! Beautifully audacious!

CHRISTINA. Try it on.

EBBA. I wouldn't dare.

Erika puts down the gown and the box and exits.

CHRISTINA. The official portraits they send to my suitors far and wide are embellishments of my face and figure. You must try it on. I know it will suit you. (*Ebba goes to leave with the gown.*) No. Here, in front of me.

EBBA. (*surprised*) In front of you?

CHRISTINA. Descartes said, "Reason later." (*beat*) Take everything off. Slowly.

Ebba obeys.

EBBA. Why are you so silent?

CHRISTINA. I'm trying to change the expression on my face, by imagining the exact opposite. (*beat*) Your fiancé?

EBBA. Jakob?

CHRISTINA. How does he look at you?

EBBA. His eyes take great liberties.

CHRISTINA. And what else?

EBBA. (*seductively*) Sometimes he joins his hands … like you now. He raises them to his chin, like you. (*almost nude*) My fiancé looks at me the way we look at swans, praising the beauty of their wings, but forbidding them to fly.

CHRISTINA. Put on the gown.

Ebba obeys.

EBBA. Is this slowly enough?

CHRISTINA. Jakob?

EBBA. Yes?

CHRISTINA. Is he proud to have you on his arm?

EBBA. Yes.

CHRISTINA. Does he know how many men envy him in the jungle of suitors? Do you enjoy knowing that you are desired?

EBBA. When he looks at me, I can show no doubt.

CHRISTINA. Do you have doubts?

EBBA. Love is made of doubts and certainties, but especially of the certainty that we will doubt.

CHRISTINA. You've taken to reasoning now?

EBBA. It's a talent one acquires in your service.

CHRISTINA. Do you like feeling desired?

EBBA. I think so.

CHRISTINA. Does he tell you that you're beautiful?

EBBA. So often, I find him tiresome.

CHRISTINA. And how does he touch you?

Silence.

EBBA. The Venetian silk merchants are the best in the world. This gown is insolent. Beautifully insolent. Ours are so sober. With our whalebone stays and stiff bodices. Our petticoats are black, our skirts are black. We feel as if we're in perpetual mourning. Shouldn't we change that? And what about the three petticoats we wear: *la modeste, la friponne,* and *la secrète.* Couldn't we sacrifice one of them? The modesty petticoat. Although, despite its name, the frivolous—

CHRISTINA. All this deafening chatter about fabrics! The care you take of your person. The attention to

your skin. And all your delicate gestures, so delicate …
Countess Sparre, you represent everything I despise in
women. Their constant need to please. As if they only
exist in the eyes of others. And their lack of confidence.

EBBA. (*hurt*) I didn't realize that I offended you so.

CHRISTINA. I don't know how to say this, I can't explain it
to myself, but I wouldn't want to change anything about
you. Not for anything in the world. Let your gestures
remain delicate. Talk about fabrics the way one recites
poetry, speak of trinkets the way one sings hymns.
I don't know what has come over me, but suddenly I feel
like devouring a whole leg of mutton.

EBBA. (*moved*) I'm blushing.

CHRISTINA. Apparently the heart is the cause of blushing.

EBBA. Did you have this gown altered for me?

CHRISTINA. I wasn't sure you would like it.

EBBA. I like it.

CHRISTINA. You'll wear it at court.

EBBA. (*ill at ease*) At court?

CHRISTINA. Didn't you say we should change fashion?

EBBA. I don't know if I dare.

Erika enters unnoticed.

CHRISTINA. Wait. (*She hands Ebba the small box containing
a pair of pink silk gloves.*) Do you like them? Tell me that
you like them! I'm ignorant of these things. I know more
about cavalry tactics.

EBBA. (*delighted*) You shouldn't have.

CHRISTINA. You like them? Really? They're from Paris. A certain Ninon de Lenclos sent them to me. She's an Epicurean. She believes in the pleasures of the flesh.

EBBA. Oh!

CHRISTINA. She has sworn she will never marry.

EBBA. Really.

CHRISTINA. She says that women and men are equal.

EBBA. What a strange person.

CHRISTINA. This is a thought from her book …

EBBA. (*reading*) "If God had seen fit to consult me, I would have advised him to place women's wrinkles under their heels."

Ebba laughs.

CHRISTINA. I'm glad that makes you laugh. I wasn't sure. I read it twice and I didn't laugh. (*Ebba slips on the gloves.*) You're shivering!

Christina tries to warm her by rubbing her energetically. Suddenly Ebba kisses her. Erika jumps to her feet, still unnoticed.

EBBA. I shouldn't have done that. I can't help myself. I wanted to show my gratitude. I shouldn't have.

CHRISTINA. The desire to kiss me is the message your eyes transmitted to your brain, and judging that this action was beneficial to your soul, your brain told your lips to do it gently.

Karl Gustav reappears. Erika hurries to announce him.

ERIKA. Your Majesty! Your cousin!

CHRISTINA. Again?

Karl Gustav kneels before her, his forehead on the ground.

KARL GUSTAV. In my despair, I find the courage to act.
 I beg you to listen to someone whose advice you will
 heed. I beg you to listen to your mother.

CHRISTINA. My mother?

KARL GUSTAV. The queen mother, *Drottning* Maria
 Eleonora, wants to see you.

CHRISTINA. Stay close to me, Countess!

4. THE TROPHY ROOM

*Maria Eleonora enters, dressed in mourning, covered with
jewels, her complexion livid from bloodletting. She is leaning
on a tall, thin albino and attempts to control the tremor in one
hand. She bows, reluctantly, before her daughter.*

MARIA ELEONORA. (*insincere*) *Drottning* Christina! Thank
 you for granting me this audience. I heard that you fell
 during the storm. I was so worried! What a scare! I pray
 that heaven will protect you for years to come, for the
 glory of our kingdom.

CHRISTINA. To what do we owe this rare visit so late
 at night?

Beat.

KARL GUSTAV. Gracious aunt!

MARIA ELEONORA. At first, I laughed. I hadn't laughed so
 hard for ages. A deep belly laugh. The kind that stirs the

most lethargic lungs. Then, my mouth went dry. That was predictable.

KARL GUSTAV. The reason for your visit!

MARIA ELEONORA. They want me to appeal to your sentiments. That's what made me laugh.

KARL GUSTAV. Listen to your mother, Christina.

MARIA ELEONORA. He told me, "Get dressed. She hasn't seen you for so long. Certainly, she'll open her heart to you." I couldn't find my crown. There are so few occasions to wear it. I put on this old gown and this battery of jewels. How do I look?

KARL GUSTAV. Marriage, my aunt, marriage!

MARIA ELEONORA. (*unconvincingly*) How can you refuse an alliance with such a fine young man? (*beat*) My favourite nephew. A great soldier. (*beat*) Strong arms. (*beat*) I don't see what more I can say.

CHRISTINA. Marriages are necessary in times of war, madam. We are working for peace.

MARIA ELEONORA. Peace! A king's greatness is measured by his conquests, not by hypocritical treaties that only give our enemies time to rearm.

CHRISTINA. Peace is a gift to a nation.

MARIA ELEONORA. Peace is when the worst nonsense is spoken. War is when we pay the price.

CHRISTINA. From now on, the true heroes will wage battles with their minds.

MARIA ELEONORA. Words, words, words!

CHRISTINA. I brought twenty-six states together to sign this peace treaty.

MARIA ELEONORA. Listen to the Minerva of the North. In the middle of the negotiations, she invades Bohemia, sacks the treasures of Prague, and then she extends the olive branch.

CHRISTINA. The conquest of Prague hastened the signing of my treaty.

MARIA ELEONORA. (*to everyone*) Thirty years of war to impose the Lutheran faith across the north of this continent, and now she is pawning her father's inheritance for her capricious whims! Peace! (*to Christina*) Once we've been lulled to sleep by your dove's song, our enemies, brandishing Rome, will rise up again and stab us in the back, the way they did your father. Is that what you want for a wife, my nephew?

KARL GUSTAV. Yes.

MARIA ELEONORA. Then I pity you!

KARL GUSTAV. You are wrong!

MARIA ELEONORA. After all these years, I hoped to see unexpected grace. (*She caresses the albino's face.*) Purity! (*to Christina*) If your father could see you now!

CHRISTINA. Let's say he was lucky to die young.

MARIA ELEONORA. Barely out of my belly, what did they bring me? Instead of another stillborn prince, they handed me a girl, ugly and alive.

Axel comes rushing in, looking like someone who has dressed hastily.

AXEL. What is going on here?

CHRISTINA. (*about to explode*) You made my father the object of your grotesque grieving. An embalmed cadaver that lay for two years on your bed. His heart in a glass case on your canopy. A pestilent, reeking corpse surrounded by your mourners and your albinos. I was six years old and you forced me to kiss that dead body, at sunrise and at sunset, every day, day after day.

MARIA ELEONORA. We swore we would be buried the same day.

CHRISTINA. You made me witness his decomposition. My father, my hero!

MARIA ELEONORA. You will never know the power of such love.

CHRISTINA. By lepers' drool, may God spare me!

MARIA ELEONORA. You cannot understand how heavy absence weighs.

CHRISTINA. Seeing you again reminds me that not every absence is a terrible weight.

MARIA ELEONORA. Your father and I—such a beautiful love. And you, such an ugly fruit …

CHRISTINA. (*shouting*) I order you to leave!

MARIA ELEONORA. You order me? Do you remember who I am?

EBBA. (*exploding*) The queen said: leave!

Time stands still.

MARIA ELEONORA. What? An irritating gown is speaking to me?

EBBA. Leave! Leave!

MARIA ELEONORA. A whore's gown is telling me to leave?

KARL GUSTAV. (*exploding, in turn*) Marriage, gracious aunt!

Descartes and Chanut enter the hall.

AXEL. This meeting has gone on long enough.

CHRISTINA. My father had nothing but scorn for you.

MARIA ELEONORA. My mouth is dry.

CHRISTINA. You were a bottomless pit of longing that terrified him!

MARIA ELEONORA. My daughter is speaking sentences and my mouth is dry.

CHRISTINA. You demanded his constant attention, even the air he breathed. The perfect way to erode desire.

MARIA ELEONORA. I have no saliva.

CHRISTINA. Devoured by jealousy, you followed him to every battlefield.

MARIA ELEONORA. Saliva!

CHRISTINA. Hounded, he left you behind in the camps and went to see his whores.

MARIA ELEONORA. Saliva!

CHRISTINA. He was only faithful to you during his two years of putrefaction.

Beat.

MARIA ELEONORA. (*gravely*) That night, at the top of the
staircase, you were whining in my arms like a puppy.
I never felt right about it, but today I have my regrets.
Oh yes, I have my regrets. I should have left you there at
the foot of the stairs where I threw you.

EBBA. (*horrified*) No!

KARL GUSTAV. (*falling to his knees*) Good Lord!

General consternation.

CHRISTINA. (*solemnly*) So it wasn't a distracted servant?
It was you?

MARIA ELEONORA. You don't know what it means to have
children. You were only two years old.

CHRISTINA. What?! Now there's an age when it's acceptable
to throw a child down the stairs?

MARIA ELEONORA. I wasn't meant to raise a child.
To provide a firm foundation.

CHRISTINA. (*sarcastic and shattered*) And my foundation
was thirty-two stairs! (*beat*) Go back and lock yourself
up in your castle, madam.

MARIA ELEONORA. One piece of advice, my daughter:
accept your duty. Open your legs. Otherwise, I fear for
your crown.

CHRISTINA. Out of my sight!

The albino leads Maria Eleonora away.

AXEL. The Council thought it best to conceal the truth –

CHRISTINA. (*to Axel*) You knew!

AXEL. In the best interests of the kingdom—

CHRISTINA. You, almost my father, you knew?!

AXEL. My child—

CHRISTINA. You, too! Get out of my sight!

Axel exits.

KARL GUSTAV. If you want to see me again, I'll be there. Before you have time to say my name, I'll be there. I will do anything to fulfill your deepest desires. If necessary, I will learn to talk astrology and physics. I will compose poems for you. Do you want me to slit your mother's throat?

Beat. He exits.

CHRISTINA. (*to Ebba*) I forbid you to cry. This is not your sorrow. (*Ebba takes Christina into her arms to console her.*) How dare you? (*Christina shoves Ebba, who falls to her knees, forehead on the ground.*) Have you forgotten who I am?

EBBA. I thought—

CHRISTINA. What did you think?

EBBA. Your affection? Our friendship?

CHRISTINA. Things said in a moment of weakness!

EBBA. You spoil me with presents, then you turn on me from one minute to the next. First I am the most fortunate of all women, then suddenly the most unhappy. First I feel as if you're confusing the devotion I owe you with another feeling, then I'm the one who feels as if I'm confusing everything.

CHRISTINA. This is the wrong time and the wrong place.

EBBA. In the same breath, you ask me to be both your
    equal and your servant. I do things that are beyond me.
    Things driven by a force I don't understand. If the queen
    says, "We shall be friends!" I must be her friend. If my
    friend is suffering, I must suffer with her.

CHRISTINA. The moments of distraction we shared do not
    give you the right to behave this way. From now on,
    consider yourself a pleasant decoration. And my mother
    was right about one thing: you look like a whore in
    that gown. (*Ebba exits. Descartes approaches Christina.*)
    The desire to strangle my mother is the message my
    eyes transmitted to my soul, which judged this action
    to be right. My soul ordered my hands to do it. To do it
    violently. And I didn't do it. By God's ass, I didn't do it!

DESCARTES. The impulse was appeased by your conscience.
    Freedom of conscience is the noblest force within us.
    You acted according to your free will. Like love, there
    are two kinds of hatred. The feeling we simply call
    hatred, which is related to things that are bad for the
    soul. And the other feeling we call horror, which is
    related to things that are ugly for the soul.

CHRISTINA. I hate my mother, who has a horror of me.

Beat. Descartes puts his hand on her shoulder.

DESCARTES. I'll leave you now.

CHRISTINA. Pursue your research. I'll make sure they
    provide the cadavers you need.

DESCARTES. Good night, Your Majesty.

*Descartes exits. Christina collapses. Beat. She becomes aware of
Chanut's presence.*

CHRISTINA. You were present? Stay! Do stay! Let's discuss trade.

CHANUT. Pardon me?

CHRISTINA. Yes! Let's talk prices! Profits! Wealth!

CHANUT. It's nighttime, Your Majesty!

CHRISTINA. Commerce doesn't bear the light of day.

CHANUT. The prospect of lasting peace opens many commercial possibilities.

CHRISTINA. (*struggling to regain her composure*) I want France to be the first to profit from our future developments. We're going to open roads. To the north. Roads everywhere. These territories shouldn't be left to the reindeer and the wolves. Our mines are rich. We will make them deep. Our forests are inexhaustible. We will cut them down to the roots. Our rivers are powerful. We will harness them with mills with gigantic vanes. For the welfare of my people. Yes, for the welfare of my people.

CHANUT. You belong elsewhere!

CHRISTINA. What?

CHANUT. You belong elsewhere. Your ideas are enlightened and modern. You have a bright and exceptionally daring mind.

CHRISTINA. Get to the point. And as you are so fond of saying: according to your protocol, this meeting never took place.

CHANUT. Your reforms are courageous, but no one here takes them seriously. Should I go on? You cannot realize your dreams under the yoke imposed by Luther. A life lived in shades of grey to merit total darkness. Should I go on? (*beat*) What can be said of your entourage? Every one of them wants to see you pregnant, subjected to the authority of a male. Should I go on? (*beat*) The construction of St. Peter's Basilica has created great effervescence. Rome is the centre of all possibilities today. The greatest minds and the most avant-garde artists have gathered there.

CHRISTINA. (*subdued*) Be brief, *monsieur*.

CHANUT. Rome needs a queen.

CHRISTINA. Rome has a pope.

CHANUT. Rome needs a virgin queen.

CHRISTINA. (*cutting him off*) And who better than the daughter of Luther's soldier? What could do more to discredit the advances of the Protestant faith than the abdication of Luther's most famous daughter? *Monsieur,* not only did this meeting never take place—

CHANUT. Our Church and the states that constitute it need your luminous mind.

CHRISTINA. —it has ended.

CHANUT. (*bowing*) Your Majesty.

Alone, lost in thought, Christina makes the crystal goblets sing.

Part Two

1. THE TROPHY ROOM

The sound of boots approaching. Johan joins Erika.

ERIKA. The sound of your boots is impressive, Count.

JOHAN. Did you really recognize it?

ERIKA. Yes.

JOHAN. So people notice it?

ERIKA. That's all we can hear.

JOHAN. And what effect does it have on you?

ERIKA. Really?

JOHAN. Yes.

ERIKA. It announces your arrival, that's all. I hope you
   don't start acting strange, too! Have you seen the aurora
   borealis? Ever since those celestial messengers began
   their dance, terrible things have been happening.

JOHAN. The servants have unpacked the lions from Prague.
   You should go see them. It will distract you.

ERIKA. I am afraid of lions, sir.

JOHAN. These lions have been reduced to straw.

ERIKA. I'm also afraid of what's inside our head.

JOHAN. How can you know what's inside our head?

ERIKA. The philosopher said.

JOHAN. What did he say?

ERIKA. He spoke of the soul and the digestion of meat.

JOHAN. Are you sure he was talking about the soul?

ERIKA. Yes. Tiny. Inside our head.

JOHAN. The soul?

ERIKA. No bigger than a pine nut. He said that love and hatred coexist inside it. Along with sadness and joy!

JOHAN. And to whom was the philosopher telling these things?

ERIKA. (*lying*) To me.

JOHAN. (*skeptical*) You're spending time with scholars, Duchess Brähe?

ERIKA. And why not? He added that we can have a conversation with God, the way we can chat with an elderly aunt or a valet. Do I talk too much?

JOHAN. Was the queen present?

ERIKA. I would prefer to be left to my ignorance, but the queen insists. I can't follow a third of what she says, and two-thirds of her explanations escape me. She forces us to read scholarly works. Mathematical formulae, poems where fish fly and trees have feelings. Reading puts me to sleep. When she asks me what I think of one passage or another, I tell her I haven't reached it yet. Or worse, I tell her that, sensing how important it is, I hope to find a quiet moment to give it more thought. I've found so many ways to hide my stupidity, I'm becoming intelligent. What I'm really curious about is the latest gossip: who is courting whom, who has betrayed whom, and which of the gentlemen might suit me.

JOHAN. Your conversation is so vacuous, it's relaxing.

ERIKA. (*letting the cat out of the bag*) Yes, sir, the queen was present, and I was listening, discreetly.

JOHAN. Did our philosopher guest say anything negative about our religion?

ERIKA. He said that Luther was wrong.

JOHAN. About what?

ERIKA. About everything.

JOHAN. Anything else?

ERIKA. Not that I can remember.

JOHAN. People who speak as freely as you always have something else to say. Make an effort. Certainly you can remember something else. Is there anything that could affect our sovereign's sacred obligations? (*beat*) Do you love our sovereign?

ERIKA. More than anything!

JOHAN. Then let us hear the latest gossip about who is courting whom and who has betrayed whom.

ERIKA. I'm afraid of what's happening between Her Majesty and Countess Sparre. The queen is spoiling her with presents. A taffeta gown. Pink silk gloves.

JOHAN. I see nothing strange about that. Might you be jealous of the favours the countess receives from the queen?

ERIKA. Their eyes, sir. Their eyes say more than their words. They look at each other like husband and wife. They touch each other like fiancées. They quarrel like an old couple.

JOHAN. Our monarch was raised like a prince, and that is the extent of the metaphor.

ERIKA. Metaphor? What does that word mean?

JOHAN. (*cutting her off*) How dare you insinuate such a thing?

ERIKA. I saw them. On the mouth!

JOHAN. You have an evil imagination, Duchess Brähe. And the answer to your question is, yes, you talk too much.

ERIKA. There are songs, as well. Songs that are popular in the provinces, and recently, in the taverns of Stockholm, too.

JOHAN. Sing one to me.

ERIKA. I don't know how to sing.

JOHAN. SING!

ERIKA. I don't know how to sing.

JOHAN. It's loathsome of you to spread such defamation.

ERIKA. It's loathsome of you to ask me all these questions!

Johan exits.

ERIKA. (*singing in a shaky voice*) "To lust, soldier, to lust, you drink, you shout, you sing and ask how a bawdy bed is made.

"To lust, soldier, to lust, let the royal tomboy show you how a pretty maid is laid."

2. THE QUEEN'S BEDROOM

Christina is alone. She picks up Ninon de Lenclos's book. Sound of boots. Johan enters. His shirt is unbuttoned and he is crowned with a stag's magnificent antlers.

JOHAN. I am in the tall cedar forest that surrounds our palace. It's snowing. (*Snow begins to fall, but only on Johan.*) I am the red deer, pensive, I savour the elegance of my stance, the magnificence of my head crowned with regal antlers. I contemplate my image reflected in a frozen pool. How handsome I am, my sister. A noise? No! A breath. Certainly cause for fear, but my image is so comforting, so soothing. How can I tear myself away? That breath, again! With effort, I break the spell and raise my head. I see you there, close to me. Dressed in black. The bow drawn and the arrow pointed at my heart. What do you want from me, my sister? Why this look? My gentle voice makes your bow quiver! You say fragments of words that echo in the air. "-ove! -ove! -ove! -han! -han! -han! -ong! -ong! -ong! -ime! -ime! -ime!" Like the nymph Echo repeating to Narcissus the end of the words she hears, you are incapable of expressing your love for me. It is unbearable. There lies the reason for your drawn bow and the arrow pointed at my heart. You want to kill me? My eye catches yours, seduces you, overwhelms you. "-ove! -ove! -ove! -han! -han! -han!

-ong! -ong! -ong! -ime! -ime! -ime!" And natural order is restored. "I love you, Johan, I have for a long, long time." I take your bow and lay it on the ground. You're breathless. You can't take it anymore. You kneel and put your arms around my long legs. A shiver runs up my spine. The tips of your breasts stiffen. You climb my long legs. Your lips on my belly. Your hair on my neck. Your hand on my round, polished shoulder. The other hand travels down, searching for the throbbing line. You tremble like a leaf beneath the first drops of rain. And I feel a rush of confused desire. A ripple of pleasure knowing that you are exploring my perfect shape. All semblance of reason abandons me. A strange, obsessive idea takes hold: I am going to fill you with me. I am going to fill you with me.

CHRISTINA. (*impressed*) By all the drunks of the wedding at Cana! What a dream, my brother! What a dream!

JOHAN. I have come to take you. It's decided. I'm going to marry you!

CHRISTINA. It's an epidemic!

JOHAN. I'm the only one who can give you the pleasure you deserve.

CHRISTINA. The what?

JOHAN. Your squeals of delight will echo to the ends of the earth.

CHRISTINA. Your author's name ... I'll have him hanged!

JOHAN. I grew up with you. I know you by heart. In fencing, you say "flank." I say "heart." You say "chest," I say "heart." I always know where you will strike.

My sister, the time has come to discover a union more powerful than the bond of childhood companionship.

CHRISTINA. Don't come so close to me.

JOHAN. Your forehead is creased with questions, I will soothe it with fulfillment. Who could be more attractive in this land than me? I love talking about myself. It makes me giddy. (*He lies on top of her, threateningly.*) You will lose your taste for reading. You will find philosophy banal. You will praise God for the joy of sharing your bed with me every night. And our children will be beautiful.

She struggles and resists his violent embrace.

CHRISTINA. By the rusty nails of the Cross on Calvary, I didn't know there was a god for the pretentious, too. NO ONE CAN TOUCH ME!

She manages to grab her dagger and threatens Johan. He removes the stag's head.

JOHAN. What are you waiting for? Go ahead! (*He tears off his shirt.*) Here. On my chest! One night turned morning in a tavern, I saw a poet armed with a dagger engrave verses on his mistress's belly. Tears filled their eyes. Tears of pleasure, tears of pain.

"Tell me, forlorn lover, what spurs your sad lament? What blow has your heart rent? You have no one but yourself to blame—for your pain and your pleasure are one and the same."

The blood from one letter dripped on another and formed a third. A new alphabet was born! And unbidden, untouched, my sex emptied its seed in long, jerky bursts. Ecstasy! Ecstasy, my sister! Go ahead.

Sharpen your blade. Compose on my belly. I say "heart," write "flank." Go ahead. Stop being a brain and become a beast.

CHRISTINA. (*sarcastic*) When am I supposed to get down on all fours and whimper?

JOHAN. (*dead serious*) Now!

CHRISTINA. And with each moan, I'll lose one divine right?

JOHAN. One or two provinces.

CHRISTINA. And for the price of my hymen, your sex will be adorned with the rings of my crown?

JOHAN. A pleasant thought.

CHRISTINA. I'll become half, a portion, a shadow, an object?

JOHAN. Half, yes, of all of that.

CHRISTINA. I'll be happy, with your permission?

JOHAN. If and when I so desire.

CHRISTINA. You don't love me, Johan.

JOHAN. Who is talking about love? You need a king. A king to show you how to guide your nation. (*beat*) Your subjects don't want to be changed. Forget your schools, your books, and your scholars. You can't drive cattle by quoting Sophocles! We need strong arms, not brains. Who is going to dig your mines? Demosthenes's disciples? Make your people dream. But be sure you dictate their dreams. Satisfy their senses, forget their minds. Give them money with one hand, saddle them with debt with the other. Epidemics, war, financial disaster. Frighten them! And make sure that God is your

42

accomplice in this venture. Clothe your messengers in
fine garments, and people will forget the message. Set
your opponents against each other. Let them get too
fat to stir. Replace every law passed with a new one
that annuls the former. Decorate your officers. Bribe
the clergy. Make the nobility rich. And be sure that the
artists and poets always perform the same litany, never
creating anything new. Treat your people like idiots and
they will adore you. Make me your king! As for the rest,
for "matters of the flesh," I'll think of someone else.

CHRISTINA. Very amusing, Johan!

JOHAN. Drop your bravado! The court and the Council have
lost patience. The State needs an heir.

CHRISTINA. I am not so inclined.

JOHAN. I don't want to believe the rumours of your
perversion.

CHRISTINA. Rumour is a weak prosecutor.

JOHAN. They say the Devil has donned a seductive shape
that will be your downfall.

CHRISTINA. And tonight, is it God who dressed you?

JOHAN. I don't want to believe in your deviance.

CHRISTINA. My what?

*Ebba enters, dressed in a severe, black gown. She is holding the
taffeta gown and the gloves.*

EBBA. Your Majesty!

JOHAN. (*pointing to Ebba*) I don't want to believe in this!
(*beat*) A woman cannot deprive herself of a man's desire

to satisfy the desires of another woman. And those who do, do so only in our presence, to increase our pleasure.

CHRISTINA. (*confronting Johan*) Johan! The nymph Echo is telling you, "Go! Go! Go! Away! Away! Away!"

Johan gathers up his clothes and withdraws.

CHRISTINA. (*to Ebba*) Look at what's happened! What a mess! Friendships with women are sentimental affairs that distract me from my duties. Pacifying Europe's religions. The signing of my peace treaty! Taking a stand on the position of the earth in the planetary system. You display your charms indecently, you pose and pout your pretty lips constantly. We say, "Take everything off!" and suddenly you stand as naked as a goddess from antiquity! Don't you realize that "everything" is relative and must be used with moderation?! Read Pascal again. We say "slowly" and you move as slowly as the chrysalis becomes a butterfly. Austerity and asceticism should be your adornments. "Subject your desire to moderation so it remains guided by faith, the supreme master of God's gifts." Read Luther again! This is what I think of your laces! (*She rips off her lace cuffs.*) Don't just stand there silent! Make some noise!

EBBA. I have come to ask a favour.

CHRISTINA. I grant it, whatever it might be.

EBBA. I haven't named it yet.

CHRISTINA. That makes this exchange all the briefer.

EBBA. Relieve me of my duties in your service.

CHRISTINA. Granted.

EBBA. I am returning your gown.

CHRISTINA. Satan's skin.

EBBA. And Mademoiselle de Lenclos's gloves.

CHRISTINA. Medusa's serpents.

EBBA. Here is one.

CHRISTINA. So be it.

EBBA. And the other.

CHRISTINA. Not more sobs! Women cry so often, it's easy to confuse their tears with perspiration.

EBBA. I'll dry my tears.

CHRISTINA. I could do without your sadness. Most of all, I could do without being the cause. I relieve you of your duties. Leave!

EBBA. Adieu.

Ebba goes to withdraw.

CHRISTINA. Take these gloves back! And leave!

EBBA. Very well.

CHRISTINA. Here is one.

EBBA. So be it.

CHRISTINA. I'm trembling like a leaf. I'm blushing red as a Dane! If Descartes were here, he could explain the meaning of this long leave-taking. By God's ass! My reason wants you to leave, my blood asks you to remain. (*Ebba withdraws again.*) Countess! (*almost inaudibly*) Hold me in your arms.

EBBA. What?

CHRISTINA. Hold me in your arms. (*Ebba takes her in her arms.*) In the winter, during the military campaigns, my father asked a nobleman to warm his bed for him. He lay in the bed before my father and the sheets were warm when the king came to join him. They called him the king's bed companion. (*Silence.*) You will have this title and assume these duties.

EBBA. I came to bid you farewell.

CHRISTINA. Forgive me for subjecting you to my anger.

EBBA. You need not ask for my forgiveness. You are my sovereign.

CHRISTINA. (*kissing Ebba awkwardly*) That wasn't very good, was it? I know how to set a bear trap, and how to take apart a musket, but … I don't know how to place my lips and … my hands are awkward and …

Ebba kisses her.

EBBA. There, that was better.

CHRISTINA. I swear, with you as my witness, that from now on I will act according to my free will, and I will judge, in my own soul and conscience, what is good and what is evil. For as long as I sit upon the throne of Sweden. You may get rid of *la modeste, la friponne*, and the secret petticoat. I'll teach you how to use a sword and a musket, how to ride and laugh out loud. Woman or man? A pointless question.

The two women begin to undress. Off to one side, Johan straightens his clothes. Axel joins him, and they observe the two women.

AXEL. Did you say the words I told you to say?

JOHAN. Narcissus's dream, the magnificent red deer, Echo, the nymph. I even imitated the echo. (*hurt*) All these years spent perfecting this splendid machine, only to be humiliated. (*exploding*) I'm talking about me! (*beat*) Her Majesty has showered Countess Sparre with presents, a gown, gloves. Countess Sparre is the most beautiful woman in the kingdom. And she has just received the title of bed companion to the queen.

AXEL. Friendship between women is subject to interpretation. There is more intimacy between them than between men.

JOHAN. When will you stop kidding yourself, my pathetic papa? You brought her up like a man and now you're surprised that she whistles at women! Where do you think she gets her insatiable appetite for knowledge, her determination to change the natural order of things? From her perversion, Father! Perverts need to question the natural order of things. They need to make the world fit their peculiar vision. The more scandalous her behaviour, the more severely we'll be blamed—and quickly overthrown.

AXEL. (*gravely*) We mustn't exaggerate.

JOHAN. The lover has appeared as a pearl. We must remove the ulcer from the shell.

AXEL. I'm not sure ...

JOHAN. Will we wait until women wear breeches and gentlemen are eunuchs?

AXEL. I'm not sure ...

JOHAN. When will we remove the worm from the apple?

The silhouettes of Christina and Ebba, dressed like men, appear in the shadows. They run back and forth, laughing, prancing. Beat. Ebba stops to massage Christina's shoulder.

CHRISTINA. Ebba? That is your given name? Sweet Ebba. Is this how Jakob caresses you? I will make him a knight.

EBBA. Jakob?

CHRISTINA. Yes. For having taught you to caress so gently. (*Silence.*) Read to me again. Your voice. Again, your voice.

EBBA. (*reading from de Lenclos's book*) "If you wish to keep a lover, you must withhold one favour every day, so you have something new to give on the morrow. Do not grant in a single day everything that can sate the appetite you have aroused."

JOHAN. (*reading, off to one side*) "Cut her hair and pour boiling alcohol on her head. Then set the fire. Her hair will burn right down to the roots."

EBBA. (*reading on*) "Diversify the pleasures, offer the charm of inconstancy."

JOHAN. (*reading on*) "Insert hooks in her back and thread ropes through them."

CHRISTINA. Tomorrow you will sit at my right in the throne room.

AXEL. Remove Countess Sparre from the court immediately.

Semidarkness. Loud knocking at a door. Johan is facing Erika. Beat. Blackout. Erika emerges from the dark.

ERIKA. (*to the audience*) The queen was happy and in high
    spirits, a mood all too rare for her. She was laughing.
    I remember that the two women were reading Ninon
    de Lenclos together. Then, between two sentences,
    Countess Sparre was there, and suddenly she wasn't.
    Someone knocked at the door. "A messenger. Highly
    important. An emergency. The countess has been called
    to the bedside of a dying relative." I was told to tell the
    queen, "A messenger. Her family. An emergency." With
    not so much as a bow or a farewell, the countess left
    the queen.

JOHAN. (*to Ebba*) Your voice. Again, your voice.

EBBA. (*terrified, holding a book*) "Insert hooks in her back
    and thread ropes through them. Suspend her from
    the ceiling for three or four hours. Then lower her
    to the floor. Crush her fingers beneath your heavy
    boots. (*Johan turns a page in the book.*) The following
    morning … (*Johan makes a crystal goblet sing and the
    sound becomes increasingly strident.*) Tie her to the rack,
    naked, and heat a blade. Place the blade on her belly and
    begin to write."

Part Three

1. OUTSIDE UPPSALA CASTLE

KARL GUSTAV. (*alone*) Ten days! Ten days since Christina
was last seen at court. For ten days, she has locked
herself up in her quarters. She demands silence from
her servants, not a word, not a sound. Not even a hymn
or a prayer. Her ladies-in-waiting are distraught. No
decrees, no laws. She didn't even sign the order for my
banishment. The State is paralyzed. (*suddenly*) I can
hear her cries. I'm the only one who hears her. They say
she goes riding in the middle of the night and doesn't
return till dawn. Wearing nothing but her nightdress.
They say she struck a page who dared look at her with
compassion. They say she is burning books, her favourite
books. They say that she is in love. Peace is madness.
This morning, they slaughtered two hundred horses
from the royal cavalry. The finest. The ones that led us
into battle. Useless. Too expensive to feed! Our army's
pride and joy in the begging bowls of the poor. They
are melting our armour. Turning it into chamber pots.
Bears are being decimated. Carnage. We have to shoot
at something. Not a single soldier lifts a sword. They're
too busy lifting their mugs. The glory of our victories is

fading as fast as the kegs are emptied. Peace is madness. We are not used to having time, time made of minutes and hours, time for feelings, for laughter and tears. I'm sure that was her cry. Deeper than the others.

I'm the one you love.

I know you don't know how to show me, I know you're troubled by this emotion that terrifies you.

I love you! I love you! I love you!

I wish I knew how to express all the ways I love you. I don't have the grammar or the vocabulary. I love you till your hair. I love you till your eyes. I love you till your lips. I love you till your hips. I love you till your shoulder. I say, "My sweet one," I think, "I want your breasts"! I say, "My beauty," I think, "Open your legs." I say, "Goddess," I think, "Goddess."

My girl king. My precious girl king.

MARIA ELEONORA. (*as she enters, sitting in a wheelchair pushed by her albino*) "My girl king. My precious girl king." Words, words, words! How tiresome!

KARL GUSTAV. It was stupid of me to ask you to intercede on my behalf.

MARIA ELEONORA. I need an escort to return to my castle. My daughter still hasn't signed her consent. I have no one to attend to me. I smell bad.

KARL GUSTAV. Very stupid.

MARIA ELEONORA. She is more inclined to spontaneity than to self-control. From birth, Uranus was a strong influence, as was the upper octave of Mercury.

The moon is the most important planet in her chart.
She is incredibly unstable.

KARL GUSTAV. You have to blame the heavenly bodies to
mask the consequences of your acts. You are cruel.

MARIA ELEONORA. My poor nephew! The pleasures of
cruelty are lost on the simple-minded.

KARL GUSTAV. You have no sense of honour or decency.

MARIA ELEONORA. I have elegance and manners. I have
goodness and generosity.

KARL GUSTAV. Oh really? You hide it well.

MARIA ELEONORA. (*indicating the albino servant*) In his
safekeeping. Nordic legend has it that a covenant with
those whose hair and skin are as white as the driven
snow frees us from the constraints of virtue.

KARL GUSTAV. (*scornfully*) Stupid superstitions. How many
albinos did you need to not feel guilty about pushing
your daughter down the stairs?

MARIA ELEONORA. What do you want from me? Tearful
regrets?

KARL GUSTAV. Just one word. A word that could pave your
way to a better eternity.

MARIA ELEONORA. Have you any idea what it means to
be an aging queen left on her own? It's not an enviable
fate. As long as he lay, even lifeless, on our bed, her
father still ensured my power. Then they came to take
him away. A mother opens her arms to comfort her
child. I opened mine to lose her. The world was at her
feet while it slipped out from under mine. Do you know
what it's like to give birth to one's own downfall?

KARL GUSTAV. Christina will lead us out of the darkness and chaos of war. Our country will know lasting peace and I will be at her side.

MARIA ELEONORA. A country at peace is a country that exploits the wars of others. A country that supplies the arms for them to kill one other. And monstrously rich, that country can devote itself to fine entertainment and to the study of noble sentiments, while composing verses about the hypocrisy called peace. She must marry, for God's sake! She must fornicate! If she dies in childbirth, at least she will have tried to embrace her destiny.

KARL GUSTAV. I need a mug of beer. No, I need a keg!

MARIA ELEONORA. If she insists upon preserving her celibacy, the Council can remove her from office. And you should drop your insistence. You will never win her heart.

KARL GUSTAV. Take care as you leave, madam, there's a flight of stairs.

He exits.

MARIA ELEONORA. She can always marry the dauphin of Denmark. The child is only three years old. She won't have to give herself to him for a long time, and when he does come of age, he'll flee the minute he lays eyes on her.

The albino servant puts his hand over his mouth to suppress his laughter.

MARIA ELEONORA. Look, here comes the Jesuit and his clown.

Chanut enters, followed by Descartes, who is staring at the heavens.

DESCARTES. Waves of purple and green. Turquoise and mauve. The Northern Lights, tumbling like the first snow of winter. Look there, the shimmer of the phoenix's wings. And there, the veil of an angel giddy from a whirling dance.

MARIA ELEONORA. Words! Words! Words!

DESCARTES. They argue. They quarrel like children.

MARIA ELEONORA. The aurora borealis exist, *monsieur*, to make madmen believe they're sane. (*to the albino servant*) Enough! Let us go find some noise elsewhere.

She exits, pushed in her chair by the albino.

CHANUT. (*looking up at the sky*) Thanks to your teachings, the queen is questioning everything. Her faith in Luther is wavering. She is agitated, she is suffering, she is rebelling. I see a crown shaking, falling, and rolling … and I can see the gates to the Vatican opening wide.

DESCARTES. More intimate feelings are disturbing her. Feelings that dare not speak their name.

CHANUT. So let them remain unnamed. Let's keep them secret.

DESCARTES. I must help her reason with this passion which despite all appearances is not beneficial.

CHANUT. Don't interfere.

DESCARTES. What?

CHANUT. Let her stray. These disturbing feelings help our cause.

DESCARTES. There is nothing Christian about these feelings, *monsieur*.

CHANUT. We know that, but what are such scruples compared to the destiny we are offering her? (*beat*) We must fulfill all her aspirations.

DESCARTES. To what ends?

CHANUT. Without bloodshed, without battles, we will lead the greatest Lutheran monarch to embrace God's true faith. Imagine! A Catholic Sweden. A Catholic Europe, from north to south, all under the authority of the pope.

DESCARTES. My daughter died at the same age that Christina became queen. Six years old. They would have been the same age today. Ever since her death, I have been trying to recreate her. I've built an automaton. A complex mechanism. I still have to perfect certain details. A nod of the head. A shifting of the pelvis. But most of all, the movement of a hand. I want the hand to extend and open palm up. And then I want to activate the elbow, like this, so the hand is placed on the chest to listen to the mechanism of the heart. (*He demonstrates the gesture.*) The fabrication of a monarch is as complex as that of an automaton. It obeys basic laws. And the first law is that he who reigns, faithfully, loyally, must serve his people. That is the driving wheel that activates the gears that turn the axle that turns the secondary wheels. And if for personal, selfish reasons, the driving wheel starts to turn backwards, the entire mechanism is derailed.

CHANUT. What am I meant to understand?

DESCARTES. (*curtly*) I am not part of your plot.

2. THE ANATOMICAL THEATRE

The doors to the anatomical theatre swing open. Chanut and Descartes are standing over a cadaver covered with a sheet on the autopsy table. Descartes is preparing the instruments.

Erika appears, in the background. Chanut goes to join her.

ERIKA. I want to attend the lesson.

CHANUT. Only the queen is allowed to attend.

ERIKA. My curiosity is boundless but, thank heavens,
it is not scientific. All these formulae applied to the
obvious. These boring explanations of actions that
come naturally, from the cradle on. Why find words
for everything? All this gibberish, these complicated
clauses: "considered from this angle," "notwithstanding
the principles of," "consequentially" … Dead authors
are quoted, but they're not here to defend themselves.
Scholars spend hours trying to understand the ocean's
waves, the flapping of a bird's wings, the movement of
the stars. Long before these erudite treatises, the sailor
knew how to ride the waves, the bird never stopped in
mid-flight to understand the flapping of its wings … it
would have fallen from the sky. Why explain the cold if
the explanation can't help us stay warm? And why know
whether blood flows in this or that direction? The Lord
covered our bodies in skin. He must have had his
reasons for hiding all that from us. But I want to attend
the lesson. I hate to miss anything. Let me in!

CHANUT. No women are allowed!

ERIKA. Why not?

CHANUT. Duchess Brähe, you just provided a brilliant
    illustration of why not.

Christina appears, pale and dressed in a black, hooded cape.

ERIKA. She has stopped eating. Yesterday, she stopped
    drinking. (*Christina goes to stand by the autopsy table.
    Erika gets a glimpse of the cadaver.*) I saw that! Under the
    sheet. Good Lord! I saw it. A body! An inanimate body.

CHANUT. You didn't see a thing, Duchess. Not a thing.

ERIKA. (*as she withdraws*) Something terrible happened to
    someone! This isn't an anatomy lesson. This is a wake.
    Good Lord! The queen is crying … crying over Countess
    Sparre? Is it my fault? "A messenger. An emergency!"
    Did I lead the countess to the gallows?

She exits, distressed.

CHRISTINA. Who is under this sheet?

CHANUT. The freshest specimen the gravedigger could find.

CHRISTINA. Who is it?

*Descartes pulls back the sheet and uncovers, except for the head,
the cadaver of a naked man.*

DESCARTES. A human being! A marvellous machine.
    Capable of the best and the worst. The essence of
    a human being is his mind whose task is to think.
    I think, therefore I am. Your Majesty, allow me to
    introduce the brain. Bring the candle closer. There you
    go. (*Christina holds a handkerchief to her nose.*) Look, in
    the centre. The pineal gland. Directly below the Sylvian
    duct, which channels the animal spirits, the very spirits
    that give birth to our passions.

CHRISTINA. The answers to all our questions lie there?

She passes a pair of tweezers to Descartes, who extracts a tiny white bead from the skull.

DESCARTES. This, Your Majesty, is the seat of the soul.

Christina passes a gleaming knife to Descartes.

CHRISTINA. (*She speaks these lines like a prayer.*) Open it. Make a small incision. No bigger than a ray of hope. Remove the endless waiting. The sounds that make us believe she has come back. Remove the empty hallways where no footsteps can be heard. The voice that haunts us. The pleasant sound of a sentence read regardless of its meaning. The perfume that lingers. The glove dropped on the bed. The trace of a tear on a powdered cheek. The ribbons, tied and untied. The charm of a name. The fluttering eyelashes. The lips. Her lips. The hand in our hair. Remove the sweet surrender. Remove the hungry flesh. Remove the yearning, the longing in our gut. Go ahead! Begin with the endless waiting! Then, sadness. Go on! Excise desire. Take this knife and free the soul from the song of crystal.

DESCARTES. *Madame?*

Axel bursts into the theatre.

AXEL. Good Lord!

CHRISTINA. My friend! Have you found her?

AXEL. (*horrified*) What is the meaning of this butchery?

CHRISTINA. Is she with you?

AXEL. You are under the spell of charlatans who are exploiting your confusion. These men take no precautions to soothe your distress. (*He grabs Chanut by the throat.*) I won't let you to make a fool of her.

CHANUT. I shall have to report this incident to my king.

Axel releases Chanut.

CHRISTINA. (*to Axel*) Have you lost your mind?

AXEL. (*sternly*) And you, have you lost all sense of self-control?!

CHRISTINA. Must I remind you of my rank!

AXEL. I am speaking to you as your father would have.

CHRISTINA. You are not my father.

Beat.

AXEL. (*hurt*) He entrusted you to me. Look at you! Look at this carnage!

CHRISTINA. Didn't you teach me that curiosity was a great virtue?!

AXEL. Within the limits of Luther's teachings.

CHRISTINA. Luther has no curiosity whatsoever.

Stunned, Axel falls to his knees.

AXEL. You just blasphemed Luther's name.

CHRISTINA. (*firmly*) We shall all be saved. Heathens and Christians alike!

AXEL. When furious flesh rebels, God's word is the only remedy to counter this rebellion. The sexual body is destined for marriage, or for chastity. By God's ass, forget her!

CHRISTINA. (*shattered*) I can't. (*She falls to her knees.*)
I can't.

Beat.

DESCARTES. (*approaching Christina*) I question the real
presence of Christ in the Host. I believe that the earth
gravitates around the sun. I believe in free will. I had to
flee my country because of my ideas. But I am free. I do
not govern a kingdom.

AXEL. There is no exile, no country that will welcome the
passion devouring you.

DESCARTES. No refuge.

AXEL. No asylum.

*Chanut takes a sealed letter out of his pocket and hands it to
Christina.*

CHANUT. Your Majesty, I bring you a letter from the pope.
His Holiness is inviting you to join him on the throne
of Rome. For the crowns of France, Portugal, Spain, and
the Holy German Empire, your arrival in the bosom of
the Catholic realm will be the greatest victory of this
century. (*The sound of ice floes cracking. All the characters,
except Ebba, enter, anxious and silent. A solemn moment.*)
The pope will meet all your demands, be they reasonable
or unreasonable. Palaces, a personal army, a pension.
Name an artist, name a scholar, he will be under your
protection. Name a project, we will execute it. The pope
will proclaim you a virgin queen.

CHRISTINA. I will be under no obligation to marry?

CHANUT. None whatsoever.

CHRISTINA. I will be free to come and go as I like?

CHANUT. You will be free to act as you see fit.

CHRISTINA. In public and in private as well?

CHANUT. In public and in private as well. (*Christina goes to take the letter.*) *Ad majorem Dei gloriam.*

Rumble of ice breaking up. The cadaver disappears. The stage becomes an immense frozen lake. The sound of a debacle.

3. THE FROZEN LAKE

AXEL. (*to Christina*) A luminous mind in the body of a warrior! My daughter, that has impressed me since you were a tiny child. I believed in your dreams of making Sweden the greatest country in the world. But the adventurer who never ceases to expand the frontiers of knowledge will eventually fall into the abyss that lies beyond the horizon. When should I have encouraged more frivolity and surrounded you with the company of ladies and sensitive men? When should I have recognized that the Devil was leading you astray? I don't know. I have too much respect for your sacred right to govern to oppose your will, but if you renounce your father's faith, the consequences will affect much more than your person. You have no successor. If you break the seal on this letter, you will invite chaos. Your subjects will fight each other to the end. Some will follow you, preferring to remain loyal to their monarch, but you must know that most will remain faithful to your father's faith and will challenge your alliance with our all-too-recently "old enemies." Many will take advantage of this upheaval to advance their own interests. It will be remembered as a civil war. Our neighbours will wipe their feet on your peace treaty and invade us. It will be

the downfall of the Swedish empire. And I will curse
the day I called you my daughter. (*He kneels at her feet.*)
I implore you, Christina, use your cleverness, which
I know can be boundless, and save Sweden.

*The other characters withdraw, except for Descartes and Erika,
who is wearing a black veil.*

CHRISTINA. (*to Descartes*) Tell me, Monsieur Descartes,
what rules the world? The ravages of love or the ravages
of hatred?

*Descartes makes gestures, almost mechanically, to accompany his
thoughts and speech. Christina does not imitate him.*

DESCARTES. You turn your hand like this. You open it.
You place it on your chest, and you listen to the uproar
inside. And then you listen to your reason.

He exits. Erika steps forward and kneels at Christina's feet.

ERIKA. Will you ever forgive me? The lie about a dying
relative that led to her own death!

CHRISTINA. Who died?

ERIKA. I've never had any sense of consequences. I don't
know what guides me. My foolish eagerness or my
eagerness to be foolish?

CHRISTINA. Who died?

ERIKA. He said your salvation was at stake. He said it was
a pious lie.

CHRISTINA. Who died?

ERIKA. Countess Sparre died.

CHRISTINA. May your tongue rot in the bellies of mad dogs.

ERIKA. Listen. A deep rumbling. From the depths of the ice.

CHRISTINA. May your name be the vilest curse that no one dares pronounce.

ERIKA. It's Count Johan who killed her.

CHRISTINA. The sound of my world collapsing.

ERIKA. I saw her corpse. And you did, too!

CHRISTINA. You say I saw her body with my own eyes? Have I lost my mind?

ERIKA. With the ambassador and the philosopher! Under the sheet.

CHRISTINA. By the sweat of Christ on the Cross! Be silent, you frilly fool.

ERIKA. It wasn't her?

CHRISTINA. I can breathe again.

ERIKA. Who was under that sheet?

CHRISTINA. Your mother. Your father! Your child! Imagine the person dearest to you!

ERIKA. It's Count Johan who—(*the sound of boots*)—here he comes!

CHRISTINA. Leave me alone with him. (*Erika exits and Johan enters.*) Johan, do you like it when I call you my brother?

JOHAN. Recently, I've learned to like it.

CHRISTINA. You know my esteem for Countess Sparre.

JOHAN. For whom? The lady who is threatening the natural order of things?

CHRISTINA. I don't know where she is. Find her!

JOHAN. Who?

CHRISTINA. Ebba.

JOHAN. How adorable! She calls her by her given name.

CHRISTINA. Bring her back to me.

JOHAN. Me? What should I tell her, if I ever run into her?

CHRISTINA. "Life is too short to love as we are meant to. Come back quickly." From the writings of Ninon de Lenclos. Mention that as well.

JOHAN. And why should I be chosen for this mission? Why this quote? From this Ninon?

CHRISTINA. You know the crooks, the cutthroats, the scoundrels …

JOHAN. … and I know their given names, too.

CHRISTINA. You alone will know how to bring her back.

JOHAN. And what will be my reward? (*beat*) I didn't hear you.

CHRISTINA. I will praise the Lord for the joy of sharing your bed every night …

JOHAN. I didn't hear you.

CHRISTINA. And our children will be beautiful.

The loud rumble of shifting ice.

JOHAN. Me, king?

CHRISTINA. If, and only if, you bring her back to me!

JOHAN. By Mary Magdalene's customers! King! Me! By
　　Lazarus's rags! What should I do? Hold you in my arms?
　　Kiss you? Kneel before you?

CHRISTINA. Bring her back!

JOHAN. She will be here in no time. I swear to you on
　　my crown.

He exits.

CHRISTINA. (*alone*) Go, my false brother. I would jump
　　from the highest peak rather than marry you. And if
　　there is a peak that could reach the altitude of your
　　vanity, it's the one I'd choose.

Snow begins to fall.

　　My country.

　　So beautiful, so vast.

　　The northern star that guides you.

　　The sun and moon that watch over you in equal shares.

　　My country.

　　Pure. Sparkling. Immaculate.

　　The scent of cedar, yew, spruce, and pine.

　　Your crystal-clear blue waters.

　　Your gigantic bears.

　　Your majestic stags.

　　Your howling wolves.

　　Your watchful owls.

My country!

So quick to feast.

So quick to drink.

Open doors.

Open hearts.

Your secret pleasures that defy scolding and faith.

And you, our Northern Lights, do you remember
my father?

The snow, he said, comes when heaven's tears catch cold.

My great country, your queen is crying cold tears.

Is it better to despise one's country day after day, or
better to leave it and love it more from afar?

Must I renounce my people, renounce my faith,
renounce my father and everything I am, in order to
become what I want to be?

*She takes out the pope's letter. All the characters return,
including Ebba. Beat. Seeing Ebba, Christina drops the letter
on the ground. All the characters withdraw into the shadows,
leaving Ebba with the queen.*

CHRISTINA. Wait! Don't say a thing! I want this moment
to last. If you only knew how I've longed for it. Seconds
reclaim their place in minutes. Waiting becomes
happiness. Let me look at you. Let me believe for an
instant that without you my life is worthless, I am
nothing, no more than the poorest pauper. I know now
that I can never be consoled of your absence, not for
a single second. I belong to you so deeply that you can

never lose me. Speak the words that will determine the destiny of my people. I am listening.

EBBA. (*speaking loudly*) And they are listening, too, in the shadows.

CHRISTINA. Where were you?

EBBA. It doesn't matter, but I wouldn't wish it upon anyone.

CHRISTINA. Did they threaten you?

EBBA. No.

CHRISTINA. Did they fail to respect you?

EBBA. No.

CHRISTINA. Show me your hands.

EBBA. No.

CHRISTINA. Your back? Your wrists? Your neck? No sign of mistreatment?

EBBA. No.

CHRISTINA. And your honour? Is your honour intact?

EBBA. In the tradition of all ladies-in-waiting, I have come to ask you to bless my marriage. (*beat*) Don't force me to repeat myself. We love each other.

CHRISTINA. You love each other?

EBBA. Jakob! My fiancé!

CHRISTINA. And you want to marry him?

EBBA. Yes.

CHRISTINA. And you are perfectly happy?

EBBA. Yes.

CHRISTINA. And you want to spend your days and
your nights—

EBBA. Yes.

CHRISTINA. For better and for worse?

EBBA. Yes. (*again, the sound of breaking ice, louder than ever*)
You hear the sound coming from below.

CHRISTINA. The roar of a deep fault.

EBBA. I realized that I was taking you away from your duty.
(*She is overcome by great sadness.*) All those austere old
men while we were separated. Sombre theologians,
sinister advisers. And I will spare you the details of my
tête-à-tête with Count Johan.

CHRISTINA. I will make you forget it all. I will make them
remember everything.

EBBA. It was a difficult but necessary trial. (*regaining
her composure*) You are the shepherd of our nation.
You asked me to be the wolf.

CHRISTINA. We will go to Rome together. We will be
happy there!

EBBA. Really? Will you dress me as a vicar?

CHRISTINA. I love you. I never told you that I love you.

EBBA. I don't love you. I had no choice. How could I have
refused your affection? You are my sovereign. I tried my
best, it wasn't easy, to show you that I loved you.

CHRISTINA. They put these words in your mouth!

EBBA. I needed no convincing in this matter. (*beat*)
I love Jakob!

CHRISTINA. You perform the lines well.

EBBA. Bless my marriage!

CHRISTINA. Refuse to be their puppet.

EBBA. For pity's sake! I don't love you.

CHRISTINA. And now, will you join them in the wings?
Will they say you played your role well? That you seemed
sincere in your refusal?

EBBA. (*disturbed*) Cracks, faults. In the depths of the ice.

CHRISTINA. I can hear their applause. Did you deliver all
their lines?

EBBA. I am getting married. Tomorrow. At dawn.

*Christina takes out her dagger and grabs Ebba. About to stab
her, Christina controls her rage.*

CHRISTINA. The desire to stab you is the message my eyes
are transmitting to my brain, which instructs me to do it
with violence …

Ebba breaks away from Christina.

EBBA. Good Lord!

CHRISTINA. (*frozen in the same position, as if time had stood
still*) If I were a man! If I were a man!

EBBA. Bless me or kill me!

CHRISTINA. Let the Devil give you his blessing!

*Ebba shows her the pink silk gloves and throws them on
the floor.*

EBBA. Take them back! Take them!

Ebba exits.

CHRISTINA. I love you! I love you! I love you!

KARL GUSTAV. (*drunk and mean*) You're repeating yourself
like a puppy lapping up a puddle. Did the wind topple
you over? The mad fury of the wind? I didn't feel
a thing. Not even a light breeze. My sovereign on the
ground? Pitifully on the ground. How does it feel to be
rejected? I was at the tavern and they were all singing at
the top of their lungs.

"To lust, soldier, to lust, you drink, you shout, you sing
and ask how a bawdy bed is made.

"To lust, soldier, to lust, let the royal tomboy show you
how a pretty maid is laid."

Tell me. How does it feel to be discarded? Is it the same
between two women? How is it? Is it less humiliating?
Tell me. You're allowed to whine, to cry and scream.
You're the queen! But bears like me, we're grotesque
when we pant our pain. Should you dare look into
a mirror, you'll be appalled by the appearance of my
nation's monarch. "I have other plans," you said.
"A country of miners, lumberjacks, and peasants."
A country of idiots! A good thing you have your idiots
to pay for your whims and feed your court of parasites.
"My people have no words, no ideas." A good thing they
have no words, I hate to think how they would describe
what is going on here! While you throb and indulge
in your emotions, you stuff your people with dreams
of Utopia. You once loved your countrymen. Do you
remember what you wanted for them? All your projects
to make our country the finest in the world? A shared

dream? Now you love only yourself, yourself. And me, the biggest idiot of them all, I love only you, only you. (*beat, suddenly tender*) Come here so I can console you. Come! My girl king! My precious girl king! (*He takes Christina into his arms, his gestures almost ceremonial. She doesn't resist.*) If you only knew how much blood I have spilled to earn this moment. Let it last. Let me count every hair on your head. (*beat*) I love you till your hair. I love you till your eyes. I love you till your lips. I love you till your hips. I love you till your shoulder! (*He caresses Christina's shoulder.*) Do you want your mother on a skewer or in a stew? (*Christina laughs.*) You need to reassure your countrymen. They need you to console them, to protect them. They need to know they will always have food in their bellies, a roof over their heads, arms to hold their children. Your people need to know that they won't have to shout to be heard. That you will answer without raising your fist. That the frailest of frail will always be protected. Your people need a loving leader who resembles them.

CHRISTINA. I want to speak to Descartes! Send for him, immediately!

Erika enters, in a sombre mood.

ERIKA. Monsieur Descartes will not be coming back. He said, "The tinkling of communion bells! Fire in my chest! Sweat on my brow! I am sweating drops of blood. Look at my forehead, pearls of yellow blood. The ink of arsenic. They are poisoning me. The tinkling of communion bells. I am being murdered with the Host. Let everyone believe I died of the cold. For the welfare of our nations, so this peace may last, they will say that I died of the cold." (*beat*) Monsieur Descartes has gone to join the celestial messengers. Monsieur Descartes is dead. (*She goes to leave.*) I almost forgot. At the very end, he said, "It is the ravages of love." As if he wanted to answer a question.

A formidable rumble from the frozen depths. Erika joins the group. Christina places her hand on her heart and listens to it beat. Her heart can be heard beating, loudly. She stands up.

CHRISTINA. Karl Gustav, the time has come for you to give me the ultimate proof of your love. (*All the characters move closer on the frozen lake. Christina is solemn.*) Ever since I inherited my father's crown, before I was old enough to understand matters of the State, you have all been telling me to choose a king to share the throne of our kingdom. I cannot blame this patriotic sentiment inspired by your desire to avoid the inevitable chaos that would have ensued if, by an act of his divine will, God chose to take my life before I produced a legitimate heir. After much soul-searching and in the best interests of my country, I have, therefore, decided to designate my cousin, Karl Gustav … as my son, and in so doing, I make him the legitimate heir to the throne of Sweden.

JOHAN. Her son?!

KARL GUSTAV. Your son?

CHRISTINA. I am leaving you everything that is precious to me.

KARL GUSTAV. But I love you!

CHRISTINA. Then give my people a thousand times the affection you saved for me.

Reluctantly, Karl Gustav acquiesces and kneels before her.

KARL GUSTAV. I swear before God and all men that I shall
   cherish this country as much as I have cherished you.

CHRISTINA. I hereby renounce all rights to this country's
   throne. I claim the right to do as I please and I absolve
   myself of my actions, both past and future. (*She breaks
   the seal on the pope's letter. The sound of ice floes colliding.*)
   Long live King Karl!

ALL TOGETHER. (*except Karl Gustav*) Long live King Karl!

*Christina exits, followed by the members of the court, except
Axel and Johan.*

JOHAN. (*livid and feverish, his shirt stained with blood,
   holding a crystal goblet*) The books! The scientific
   instruments. The treaties and the maps. The tapestries.
   The Caravaggios and the Raphaels! She is taking it all
   with her! Five caravels. Two hundred wagons loaded to
   the hilt. This isn't an exile, this is plunder! She curses
   Luther and she leaves with a quarter of Sweden's
   fortune. A fine outcome! She negotiates her freedom
   by taking advantage of the weeping bear's blind love
   for her! She becomes his mother. He becomes her
   son! He becomes king! And I become nothing. A fine
   outcome, my father. The coward abandons her country,
   she betrays her faith and her father. Can you hear the
   bells of Rome mocking us? She didn't want to give
   herself to a man. And now she is off to kiss the ring of
   the most powerful man of all. I hope the pope enjoys her
   company! She has a lifetime ahead of her, enough time
   to piss off all of Christendom!

AXEL. By making Karl Gustav her king, she saved Sweden!

JOHAN. To hell with Sappho's disciple.

AXEL. She called upon that thing … free will, the ability to determine one's destiny oneself.

JOHAN. (*smashing the goblet*) To hell with the lesbian!

Johan collapses.

AXEL. What's wrong? Is that blood on your shirt?!

Axel takes Johan into his arms and opens his shirt.

JOHAN. She had them engrave her farewell message.

AXEL. (*reading from his son's belly*) "Our conscience is the only mirror that flatters no one." Help! Someone, help!

Deafening sound of church bells.

Epilogue

On a crystal-clear block of melting ice.

France. The convent in Lagny. Summer.

The sound of nuns chanting in Latin. Christina, radiant, removes her dark cape. She is wearing a man's vest and a blue velvet skirt and is holding one hand behind her back, hiding something.

CHRISTINA. I am so happy to meet you! The nuns greeted me like a saint. You are so lovely. Those ribbons in your hair. The way you raise your hand to your neck. In the Vatican, the pope kept his promises. There was a year of celebrations. But it wasn't long before my appearance, my cursing, and my impertinence offended Roman nobility. The pope said that I might have converted in my thoughts but not in my heart. He thought it best to send me away for a while. Here I am in France at last! I saw Paris. They prepared a triumphal arrival for me, with seven thousand horsemen and feast after feast! Your king, young Louis XIV, attended a masquerade ball incognito. He wanted to see the Amazon of the North. He made a beautiful speech. He took his time praising my intelligence and my erudition. I replied that his compliments came as a surprise, since it is well-known that the best way to appear ridiculous at the French court is to be a learned lady. A woman versed in wit and wisdom is mocked. There is no end to the gossip. With no regard for her audaciousness, she is ostracized for daring to have an opinion. And I added, "I have heard that the woman they call Our Lady of Love, Mademoiselle Ninon de Lenclos, is rotting in a convent cell. By God's ass, is this the fate France reserves for the friend of La Fontaine and Racine? Is this the fate you would reserve for me? Instead of accusing her of expressing her opinions, she has been shut away on the grounds that she ate a chicken thigh during Lent. What a cowardly accusation! All the more cowardly when one knows how the clergy gorges on thighs of all sorts, year-round. And we know how the very same clergy plots to conquer the world!" I am happy to meet you, Mademoiselle de Lenclos. I am happy to bring news of your release. At my request, the king has pardoned you. In exchange, I would like you to take back a present you sent me many years ago. (*She hands her the pink silk gloves.*) I gave them to someone who was dearer to me than everything in this world. I recently learned that she died in childbirth, before I ever knew the true nature of her feelings for me. People say that I am freer than anyone has ever been. They say I have accomplished something no man or no woman has ever accomplished. I won the freedom to obey no one, not even God, to whom I attributed the visage I chose. They say that this freedom is worth more than governing the entire world. Take back these gloves and perhaps I shall be truly free. Take them back, I beg of you. Take them!

ACKNOWLEDGEMENTS

In writing this play, I received the support of the first
"Bourse à la création Jean-Louis Roux" at Théâtre du
Nouveau Monde, the dramaturgical workshop program
at Centre des auteurs dramatiques (CEAD), under the
supervision of Élisabeth Bourget, and the playwrights'
retreat at the Stratford Shakespeare Festival, under the
direction of Robert Blacker and Bob White.

My thanks to Serge Denoncourt, my faithful ally,
and to his entire team, most especially to Céline Bonnier,
the guiding light in this adventure, to Eric Bruneau and
Catherine Bégin. My thanks also to Lorraine Pintal and the
team at Théâtre du Nouveau Monde.

And very special thanks to Évelyne Brochu, Dominique
Lafon and Louis Gravel.

This play is freely inspired by the screenplay for
the feature film *The Girl King* (written by Michel Marc
Bouchard, directed by Mika Kaurismäki).

Linda Gaboriau is an award-winning literary translator based in Montreal. Her translations of plays by Quebec's most prominent playwrights have been published and produced across Canada and abroad. In her work as a literary manager and dramaturge, she has directed numerous translation residencies and international exchange projects. She was the founding director of the Banff International Literary Translation Centre. Gaboriau has twice won the Governor General's Award for Translation: in 1996, for Daniel Danis's *Stone and Ashes*, and in 2010, for Wajdi Mouawad's *Forests*.

Quebec playwright **Michel Marc Bouchard** emerged on the professional theatre scene in 1985. Since then he has written twenty-five plays and has been the recipient of numerous awards, including, in June 2012, the prestigious National Order of Quebec for his contribution to Quebec culture, and, in 2005, the Order of Canada. He has also received le Prix Littéraire du Journal de Montréal, Prix du Cercle des critiques de l'Outaouais, the Governor General's Performing Arts Award, the Dora Mavor Moore Award, and the Chalmers Award for Outstanding New Play. Translated into nine languages, Bouchard's bold, visionary works have represented Canada at major festivals around the world.